Jessica Goes Swimming

THE
DREAMWORK
COLLECTIVE

This edition was published by The Dreamwork Collective

The Dreamwork Collective LLC, Dubai, United Arab Emirates

thedreamworkcollective.com

Printed and bound in the United Arab Emirates by Al Ghurair Printing & Publishing

Text © Jessica Smith, 2022

Illustrations © Hasīna Shafad, 2022

Design © Alexandra Andrieș, 2022

ISBN 978-9948-7644-1-0

MC-02-01-7392898

Age Classification E

The content of this book is appropriate according to the age classification system issued by the Ministry of Culture and Youth.

All rights reserved. No part of this publication may be reproduced, stored, or transmitted in any form or by any means, electronic, mechanical, photo-copying, recording, or otherwise, without prior permission of the publishers.

The right of Jessica Smith to be identified as the author of this work has been asserted and protected under the UAE Copyright and Authorship Protection Law No. 7.

Dedicated to my beautiful children,
who inspire me every day to be a better version of myself.

And to everyone who has been made to feel as though
their differences were anything but a superpower . . .

Your differences are what illuminates this world.

Jessica Goes Swimming

written by Jessica Smith
illustrated by Hasīna Shafad

THE
DREAMWORK
COLLECTIVE

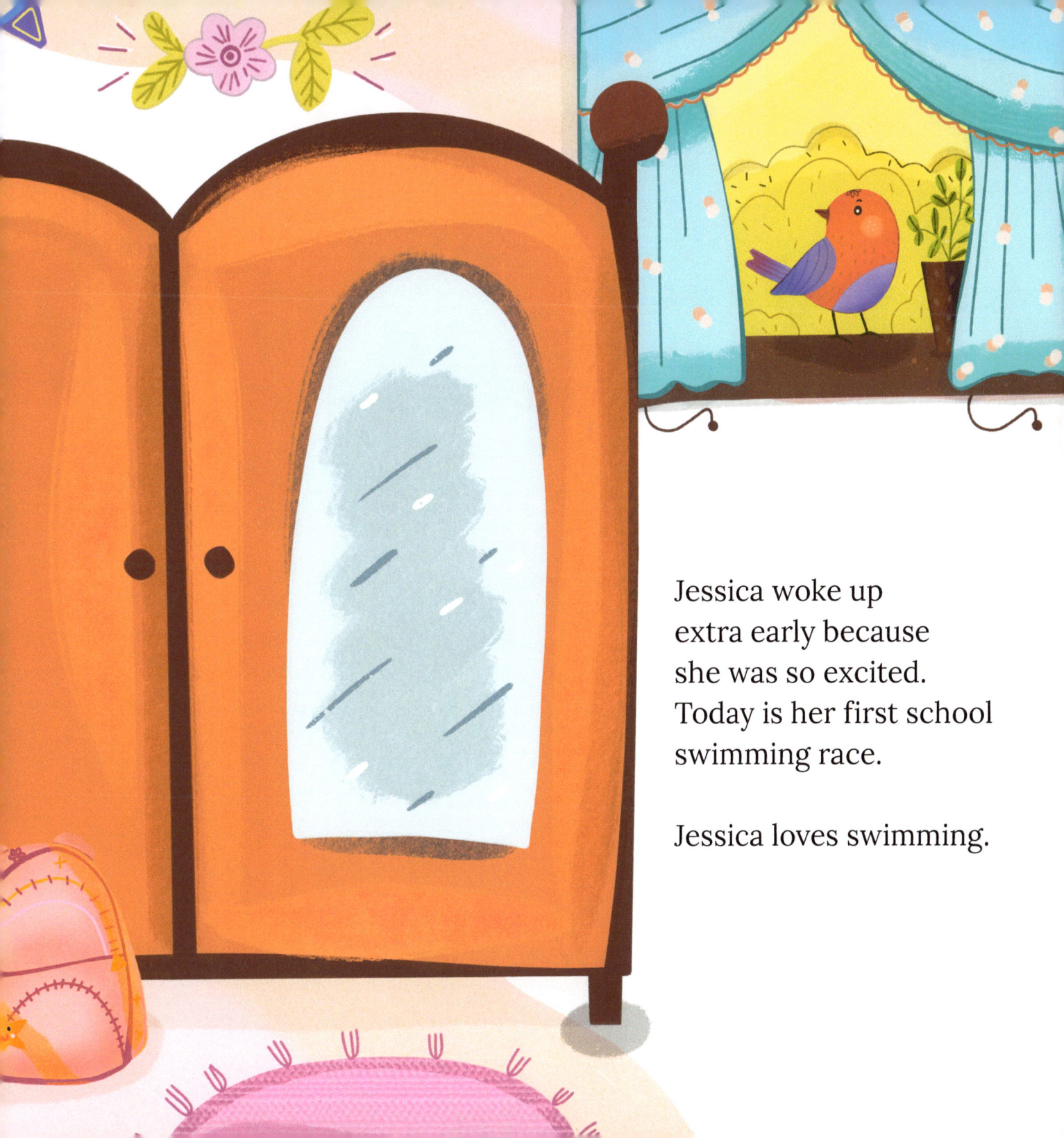

Jessica woke up extra early because she was so excited. Today is her first school swimming race.

Jessica loves swimming.

She ran to her wardrobe and pulled out her favourite swimsuit. It had blue waves like the ocean on it.

Jessica's brothers were downstairs eating pancakes for breakfast.

"Are you excited about your first school swimming race?" asked mum.
"Yes! I'm so excited,
I love swimming," said Jessica.

"Are you going to go out only wearing your swimsuit?" asked mum.
"Don't be silly, of course not!" exclaimed Jessica.

Once Jessica had finished eating her breakfast, the school bus arrived to take everyone to the local swimming pool.

Jessica's brothers ran to the front door shouting, "Good luck!"

"Don't forget your goggles," said mum.

On the way to the pool all the kids were excited and talking about who they thought was going to win.

"I'm a great swimmer," shouted James, "I'm going to win!"

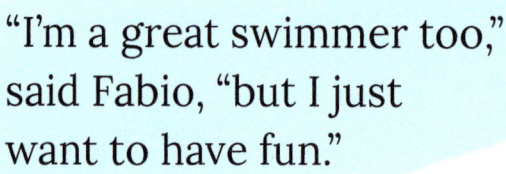

"I'm a great swimmer too," said Fabio, "but I just want to have fun."

"I can swim really fast," boasted Jessica, "maybe I'll win the race."

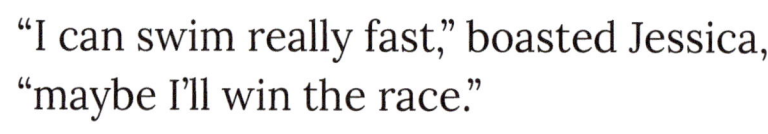

"No way!" shouted James.

"You only have one hand, you can't swim."
"Yes, I can!"
declared Jessica.

"No, you can't," whispered Zahra.

Jessica started to feel upset.
"I CAN swim!" she thought to herself.

"Don't worry," said Jessica's friend Fabio.
"Just remember to believe in yourself.
Do you love swimming?" he asked.
"Yes," said Jessica.
"Then just have fun,
you know you can do it."

When they arrived at the pool there were streamers and banners everywhere.

Jessica remembered what Fabio had said. She had to believe in herself and just have fun.

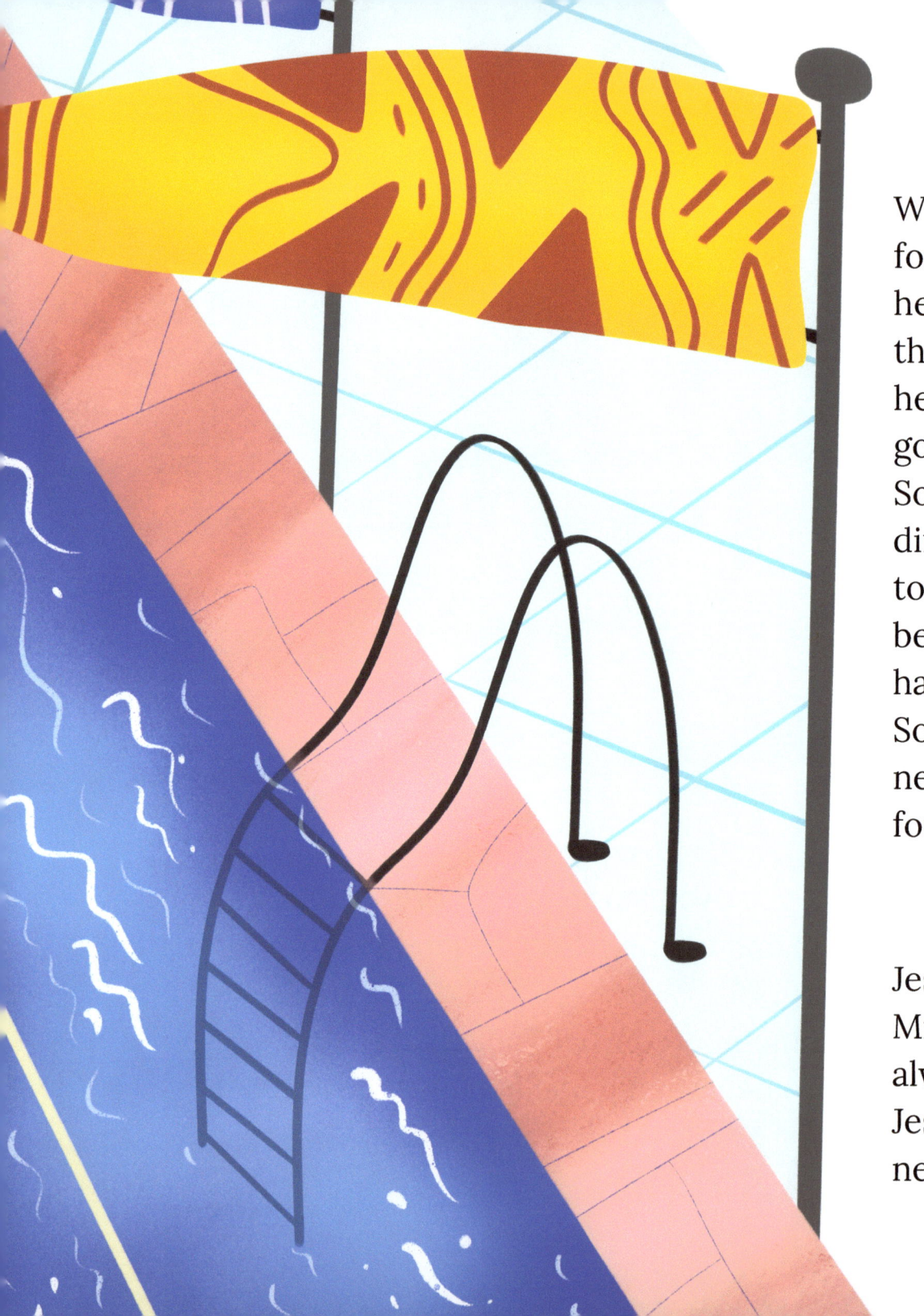

When it was time for Jessica to swim her race she realised that she needed help getting her goggles on. Some things were difficult for Jessica to do by herself because she only had one hand. Sometimes she needed to ask for help.

Jessica's teacher Miss Fitzgerald was always happy to help Jessica if she needed it.

"There you go,"
said Miss Fitzgerald,
"now go and have fun."

"I CAN do this," Jessica thought to herself.

BANG

The starter gun went off!
The race had begun.

Jessica was nervous, but excited too.
She swam faster than she had ever swum before.
"I CAN win!" she told herself.

Jessica's hand hit the wall. When she looked up she realised she had WON.

Jessica's friends Sara and Fabio
were so impressed.

"Jessica, you won!
You were right, you CAN swim fast!"

"Thank you," said Jessica,
"I love swimming, it's so much fun."

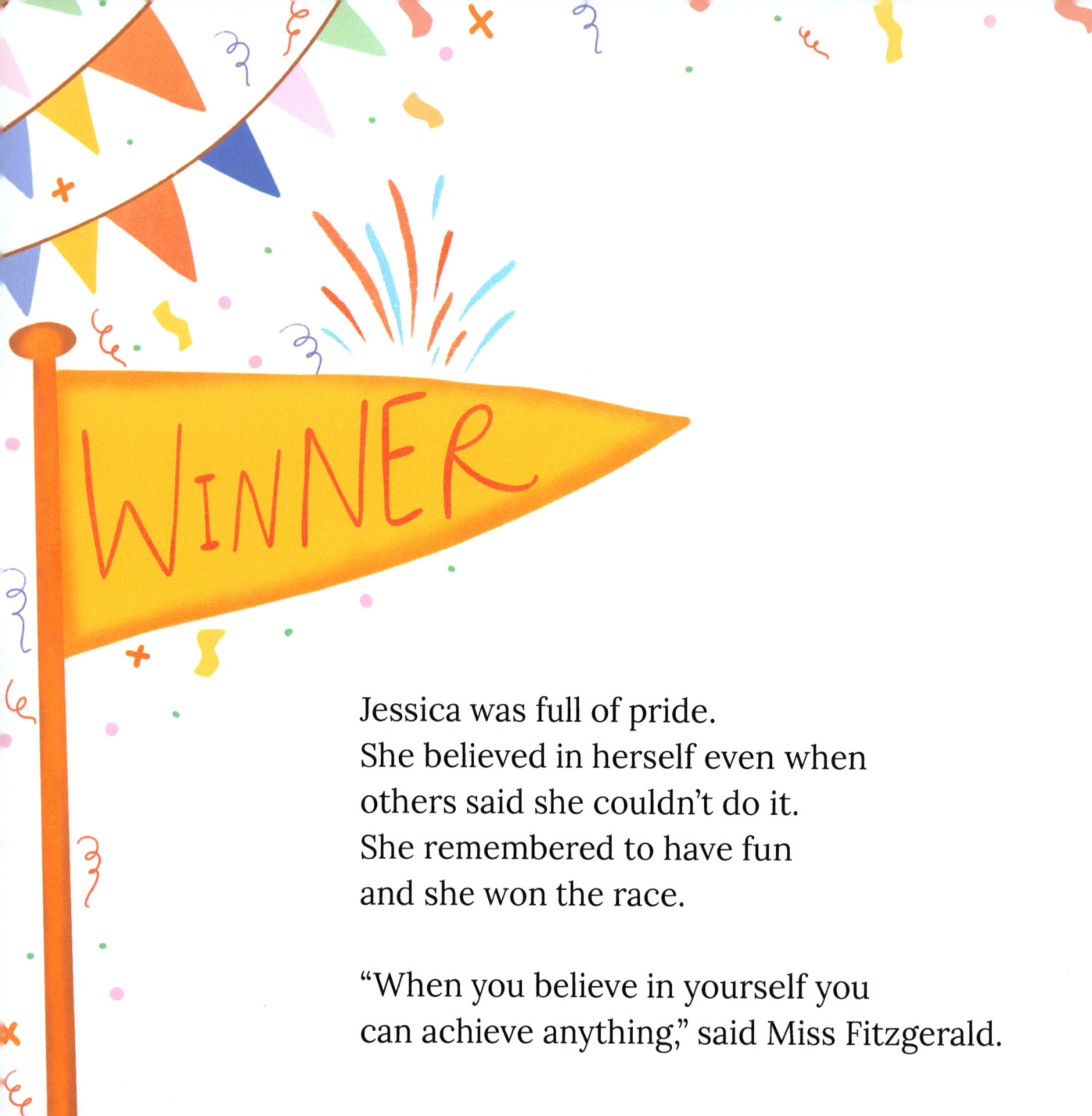

Jessica was full of pride.
She believed in herself even when
others said she couldn't do it.
She remembered to have fun
and she won the race.

"When you believe in yourself you
can achieve anything," said Miss Fitzgerald.

When Jessica got home, she was so excited to tell her parents about her win.

"How was your day?" asked Mum.
"My day was great. I love swimming so much!
I won my first school swimming race!" said Jessica.

"I'm so proud of you," said Mum.

"Did you learn anything today?" asked Dad.

"I sure did," said Jessica. "I learnt that it's important to believe in myself and to always have fun."

the end

Continue the conversation...

What's something you love to do?

Also in the *Just Jessica* series:

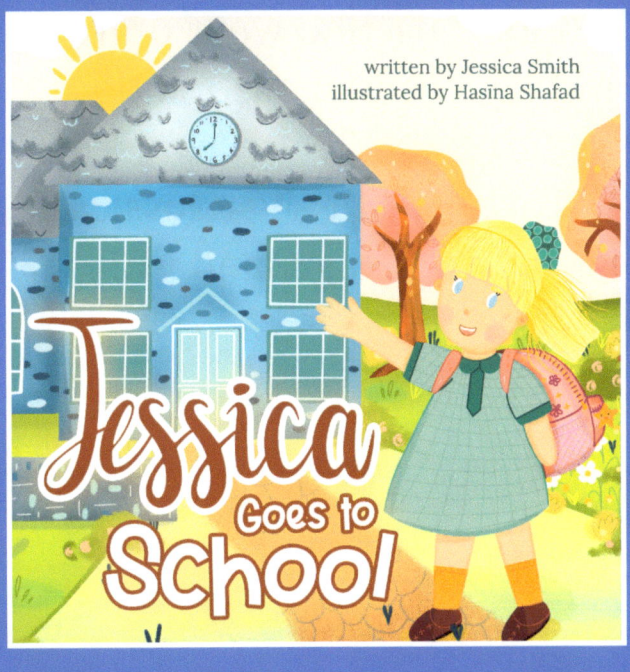

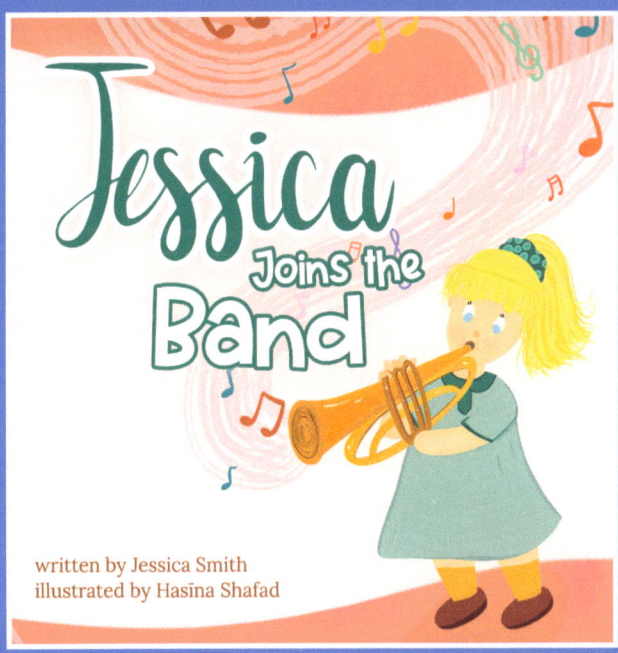

Author Bio – Jessica Smith

Jessica was born and raised in Australia, but now calls Dubai home. Born missing her left arm, Jessica focused her energy on sport and exercise as a way of proving to the world that she could overcome perceived limitations. She went on to become a Paralympic swimmer and represented Australia for 7 years. Jessica is now an internationally recognised inclusion and diversity expert. Through the Just Jessica series, the mother of 3 wants to encourage important conversations about the beauty of difference.

 @jessicasmith27

Illustrator Bio - Hasīna Shafad

Hasīna is an illustrator and artist based in Dubai. From cute stickers to wedding stationery and children's books, she loves to create colourful and cozy art that reflects the world around her. When she is not working, she enjoys reading, traveling, cooking and spending time with her beautiful family.

 **@turquoiseluna**

Publisher – The Dreamwork Collective

The Dreamwork Collective is a print and digital publisher sharing diverse voices and powerful stories with the world. Dedicated to the advancement of humanity, we strive to create books that have a positive impact on people and on the planet. Our hope is that our books document this moment in time for future generations to enjoy and learn from, and that we play our part in ushering humanity into a new era of heightened creativity, connection, and compassion.

@thedreamworkcollective

www.ingramcontent.com/pod-product-compliance
Lightning Source LLC
LaVergne TN
LVHW070447070526
838199LV00037B/712